En el bosque vive un mono.
Su nombre es Mono.

¡Hola, Buenos días!
Me llamo Mono.

Un lunes el mono come una flor multicolor.

El mono no está bien.

El martes el mono come unos guisantes.

los guisantes

¡Cambia de color!

El mono se pone de color...

verde

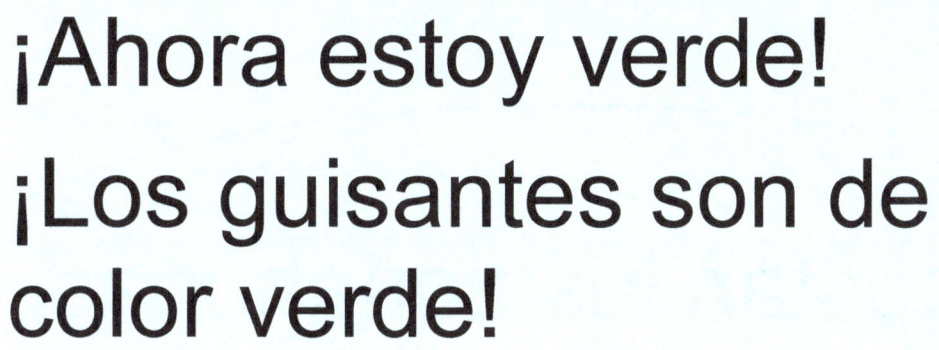

El miércoles come una zanahoria.

¡Cambia de color!

El mono se pone de color...

naranja

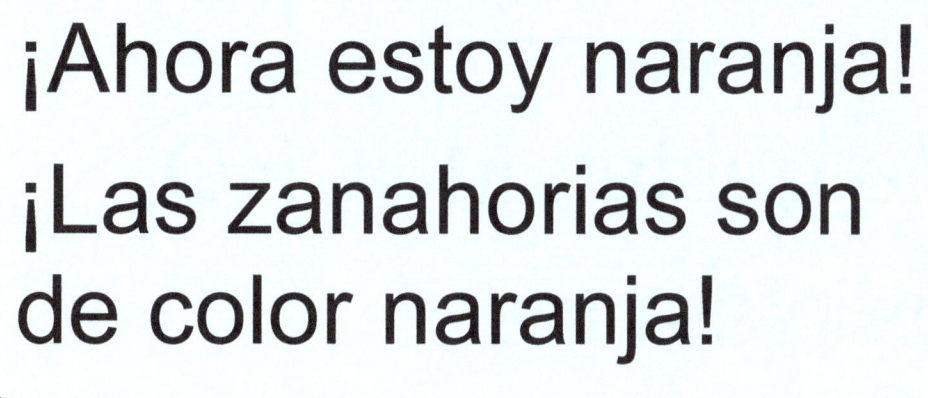

El jueves come un plátano.

¡Cambia de color!

El mono se pone de color....

¡Cambia de color!

El mono se pone de color

rojo

¡Rojo es el color de las fresas!

El sábado come unos champiñones.

"Me gustan los champiñones."

los champiñones

¡Cambia de color!

El mono se pone de color...

¡Blanco es el color de los champiñones!

¡Qué problema!

Si come los guisantes,
el mono se pone **verde**.

Si come las zanahorias,
el mono se pone **naranja**.

Si come los plátanos,
el mono se pone **amarillo**.

Si come las fresas,
el mono se pone **rojo**.

Si come los champiñones,
el mono se pone *blanco* .

El domingo el mono come chocolate.

¡Cambia de color!

I hope you have enjoyed this story! Try to look back at the Spanish words from time to time to help you remember them. Reviews help other readers discover my books so please consider leaving a short review on the site where the book was purchased. Your feedback is important to me. Thank you! And have fun learning Spanish! It's a lovely language to learn! Joanne Leyland

© Copyright Joanne Leyland 1st edition 2016 2nd edition 2018 3rd edition 2019 4th edition 2021
The useful Spanish words and phrases, the song lyrics and the translation of the story may be photocopied by the purchasing individual or institution for use in class or at home. The rest of the book may not be photocopied or reproduced digitally without the prior written agreement of the author.

Spanish

En el bosque vive un mono.
Su nombre es Mono.
¡Hola, Buenos días!   Me llamo Mono.
Un lunes el mono come una flor multicolor.
El mono no está bien.
¿Cómo estás?   Mal

El martes el mono come unos guisantes.
Me gustan los guisantes.
¡Cambia de color!
El mono se pone de color verde.
¡Ahora estoy verde!
¡Los guisantes son de color verde!

El miércoles come una zanahoria.
Me gustan las zanahorias.
¡Cambia de color!
El mono se pone de color naranja.
¡Ahora estoy naranja!
¡Las zanahorias son de color naranja!

El jueves come un plátano.
Me gustan MUCHO los plátanos.
¡Cambia de color!
El mono se pone de color amarillo.
¡Ahora estoy amarillo!
¡Los plátanos son de color amarillo!

El viernes come unas fresas.
Me gustan MUCHO las fresas.
¡Cambia de color!
El mono se pone de color rojo.
¡Rojo es el color de las fresas!

El sábado come unos champiñones.
Me gustan los champiñones.
¡Cambia de color!
El mono se pone de color blanco.
¡Blanco es el color de los champiñones!

¡Qué problema!
Si come los guisantes, el mono se pone **verde**.
Si come las zanahorias, el mono se pone **naranja**.
Si come los plátanos, el mono se pone **amarillo**.
Si come las fresas, el mono se pone **rojo**.
Si come los champiñones, el mono se pone **blanco**.

¿De qué color quieres ser?
MARRÓN
Pues come algo marrón
El domingo el mono come chocolate.
¡Cambia de color!
Me gusta el chocolate.
¡Ahora estoy marrón!

English

In the forest lives a monkey.
His name is Monkey.
Hello! My name is Monkey.
One Monday the monkey eats a multi-coloured flower
The monkey doesn't feel well.
How are you? I'm not well.

On Tuesday the monkey eats some peas.
I like peas.
He changes colour!
The monkey becomes green.
Now I'm green!
Green is the colour of peas!

On Wednesday he eats a carrot.
I like carrots.
He changes colour!
The Monkey becomes orange.
Now I'm orange!
Orange is the colour of carrots!

On Thursday he eats a banana.
I like bananas a lot.
He changes colour!
The Monkey becomes yellow.
Now I'm yellow!
Yellow is the colour of bananas!

On Friday he eats some strawberries.
I like strawberries a lot.
He changes colour!
The Monkey becomes red.
Red is the colour of strawberries!

On Saturday he eats some mushrooms.
I like mushrooms.
He changes colour!
The Monkey becomes white.
White is the colour of mushrooms!

What a problem!
If he eats peas, the monkey is green.
If he eats carrots, the monkey is orange.
If he eats bananas, the monkey is yellow.
If he eats strawberries, the monkey is red.
If he eats mushrooms, the monkey is white.

What colour do you want to be?
BROWN
Well, eat something that's brown.
On Sunday he eats some chocolate.
He changes colour!
I like chocolate.
I'm brown again!

© Copyright Joanne Leyland - This page may be photocopied by the purchasing individual or institution for use in class or at home

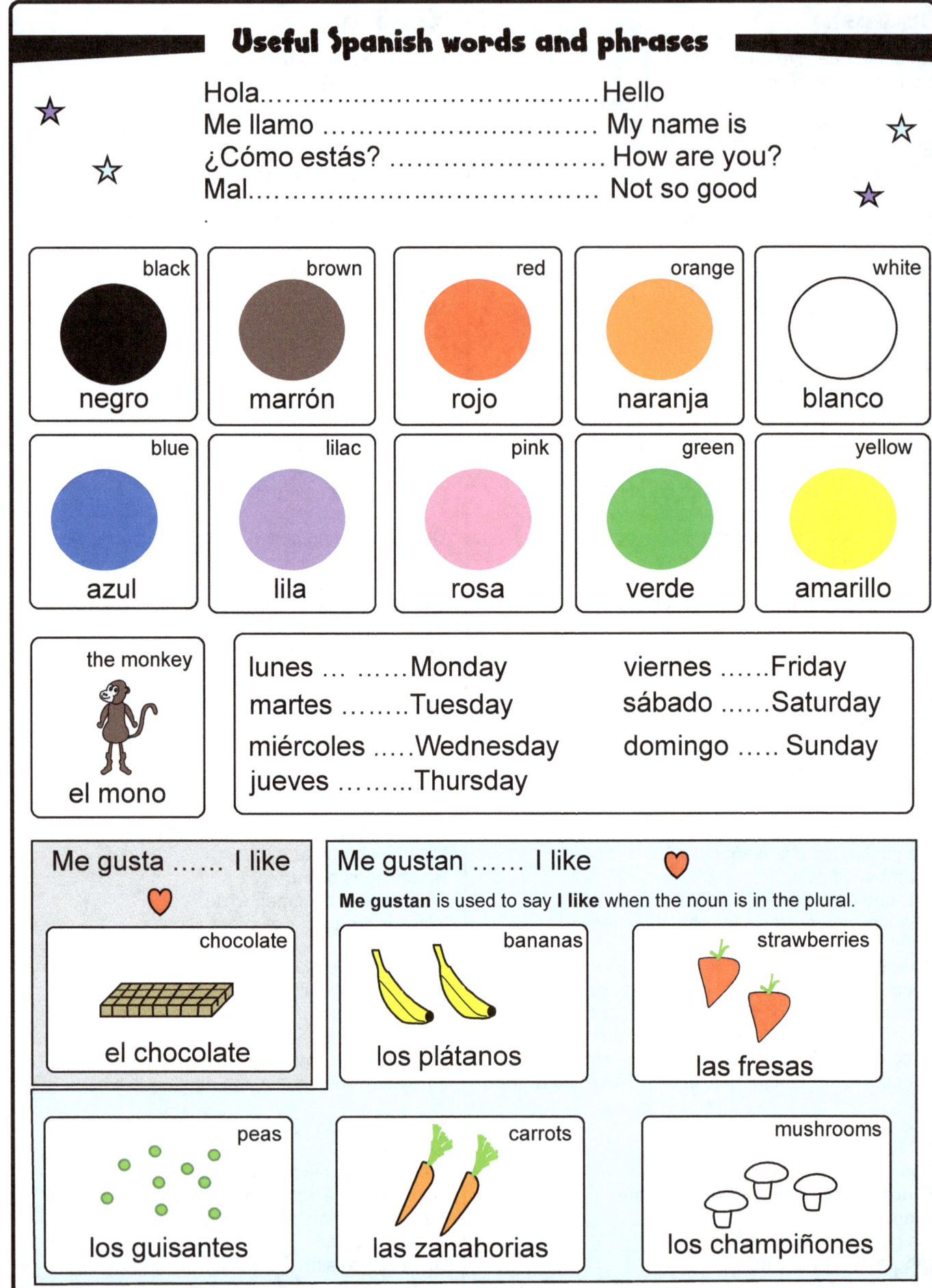

Let's sing a song!

The following words could either be sung to a made up tune, or you could try saying the words as a rap.

For inspiration of a melody to use you could hum first a nursery rhyme. How many different versions can you create using the lyrics?

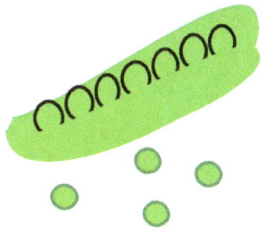

Me gustan los guisantes
Me gustan los guisantes

Me gustan los plátanos
Me gustan los plátanos

Me gustan las fresas
Me gustan las fresas

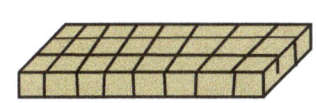

Me gusta el chocolate
Me gusta el chocolate

Follow on activity:

In the story the monkey changes to many different colours. Can you remember the correct order of the colours he turns?

rojo   verde   blanco   marrón   naranja   amarillo

Check your answers by looking through the book.

© Copyright Joanne Leyland - This page may be photocopied by the purchasing individual or institution for use in class or at home

For children learning Spanish there are also the following books by Joanne Leyland:

Un Extraterrestre En La Tierra

An alien visiting Earth is curious why there are so many things.
Topics: General conversation, clothes, weather, activities.

Seis Mascotas Maravillosas

Marcos doesn't have a pet. Will his wish for a pet come true?
Topics: Types of pets, colours, sizes, names of pets, opinions.

Spanish At Christmas Time

Bursting with fun Christmas themed activity pages, word searches, colour by number, board games, Christmas cards to make and bookmarks to colour. Photocopiable.

Spanish Word Games

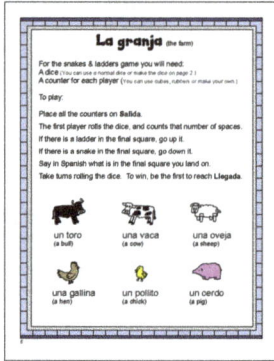
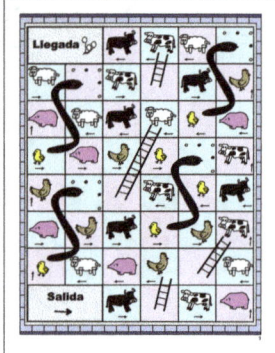

Have fun learning Spanish with this lovely collection of games. The 15 topics include fruit, the farm, ice creams, pets, hobbies, the restaurant, tapas, weather, vegetables…

Photocopiable Games For Teaching Spanish

Differentiated activities for children of various abilities. The games are colour coded according to the amount of Spanish words in each game. Games include: board games, dominoes, snakes and ladders, mini cards, 3 or 4 in a row and co-ordinates.

Topics include:
- Drinks
- Greetings
- Fruit
- Pets
- Clothes
- Food
- Transport
- Weather

For more information about learning Spanish and the great books by Joanne Leyland go to https://funspanishforkids.com

www.ingramcontent.com/pod-product-compliance
Lightning Source LLC
Chambersburg PA
CBHW081359080526
44588CB00016B/2550